How to Grow Rich with The Power of Leverage

Accelerated Wealth Creation Blueprint, for the Success you truly deserve!

By Praveen Kumar & Prashant Kumar

Disclaimer

The advice contained in this material might not be suitable for everyone. The author obtained the information from sources believed to be reliable and from his own personal experience, but he neither implies nor intends any guarantee of accuracy.

The author, publisher and distributors never give legal, accounting, medical or any other type of professional advice. The reader must always seek those services from competent professionals that can review their own particular circumstances.

The author, publisher and distributors particularly disclaim any liability, loss, or risk taken by individuals who directly or indirectly act on the information contained herein. All readers must accept full responsibility for their use of this material.

All pictures used in this book are for illustrative purposes only. The people in the pictures are not connected with the book, author or publisher and no link or endorsement between any of them and the topic or content is implied, nor should any be assumed. The pictures are only licensed for use in this book and must not be used for any other purpose without prior written permission of the rights holder.

Table of contents

Introduction

The power of leverage is perhaps one of the most neglected and misunderstood areas of an average person's knowledge. One fact will become very clear if you are to study the lives of the most successful people around you; these people, without fail, apply the principle of leverage and use it to maximum effect in their life.

Archimedes used to say, *"Give me a place to stand and with a lever I will move the whole world."* This illustrates the awesome power of leverage. Big doors swing on little hinges.

Leverage simply means '**the ability to do more with less**'. Leverage is the power to achieve a lot with little or no effort. Simply put, leverage is the key to building wealth.

To create wealth in large amounts, in little time, one has to understand and master the principle of leverage. Correct application of leverage breaks through the barrier of 10% growth/ yield. With leverage, we can grow at 50% or 60%, and even 100% or more.

Leverage, when combined with the principle of compounding, can create accelerated wealth. No great wealth has ever been created without using either leverage or compounding. Those two, when combined, together can explode your wealth. Let us examine how leverage works in the financial world.

Compounding + Leveraging = Accelerated Wealth

Robert Kiyosaki, in his book, Rich Dad Poor Dad remarks, *'if you want to become rich, you need to work less, and earn more. In order to do that, you employ some form of leverage.'*

He further explains by saying, *'People who only work hard have limited leverage. If you're working hard physically and not getting ahead financially, then you're probably someone else's leverage.'*

'People with leverage have dominance over people with less leverage.' In other words, just as humans gained an advantage over animals by creating leveraged tools, similarly, humans who use these tools of leverage have more power over humans that do not. Saying it more coherently, *'leverage is power'.*"

Types of Leverage

There are not one but several types of leverage that can be used to grow rich sooner. I will start with financial leverage, which is the most common one, and subsequently explain the other forms of leverage that help make you very successful.

Financial Leverage

Irrespective of whether you are a businessman or an investor, you need fund to grow. Everyone starts with personal funds, but these run out sooner than later. To create wealth one has to borrow from relatives, friends, banks, financial institutions or public ones. In other words, we have to work with '**Other People's Money**' or **OPM**.

The borrowed funds have to be productively employed to earn a higher return than the interest payable. Banks do this all the time. They borrow money from us at a lower interest rate and then give out loans to businesses and property mortgages at a much higher interest rate. They pocket the difference and create millions of dollars in profit.

If you have money sitting in the bank in your savings account or retirement account, then others are using your money as their leverage'.

To create wealth, you have to think like a bank. You have to use Other People's Money to grow.

To explain this point, let us see how leverage works in real estate. Let us say you buy an investment property for $100,000 at 10% down payment. This means that you make a down payment of $10,000 and borrow $90,000 from the bank. Let us assume that the rent from the property covers the interest and expenses on the property. If the value of that property increases by 7% over the year then the property would be worth $107,000. This would mean that your investment of $10,000 has earned a whopping return of $7000 or 70% yield.

This happens because you get to leverage not only on your investment of $10,000 but also on the borrowed amount of $90,000. There are sophisticated property investors who buy property with 'no money down' or very little of their own money i.e. they work on 100%

borrowed funds. In this case, the return on investment will be infinity.

Borrowing money and creating debt is good if the funds are utilized intelligently to create wealth through business and investment. The profits need to exceed the cost of borrowing. A debt created for consumption purposes: for buying luxury items such as cars, television, etc. is bad debt. Such debts take money out of our pockets and have to be treated with great caution.

Good debts make us rich. Poor debts make us go broke. The power of leverage in finance, when applied correctly, can make us grow rich exponentially.

Leverage of Knowledge

Perhaps the leverage of knowledge is the greatest lever that a person can apply. Your wealth creating ability depends on what lies between the two ears. One has to develop financial muscles in the brain. Intellectual leverage is the most powerful leverage. **I have seen entrepreneurs amass massive wealth with nothing more than an idea**.

"Thinking is hard work. When you are forced to think, you expand your mental capacity. When

you expand your mental capacity, your wealth increases." – **Robert Kiyosaki**

The fastest method to achieve intellectual leverage is to use '**Other People's Experience'** or **OPE**. It takes too long to learn on your own—become an apprentice and find a mentor. Learn from the experiences of those who have travelled the path.

Secondly, knowledge has become so complex that no lone individual can acquire all the knowledge one needs to grow rich. Wealth is created through knowledge or ideas of other people. One has to learn the art of using '**Other People's Ideas'** or knowledge. This may require collaboration or buying the right expertise to cover any grey areas that exist in our knowledge construction.

What is needed by a wealth creator is the judgment—as to what knowledge is needed for a particular project and from where it can be imbibed at the cheapest price. Our world is full of specialists who do not know how to apply their knowledge to create wealth. It is wealth creators who leverage the knowledge of the specialist to amass great wealth.

You have to develop a keen eye for talent and look out for skillful people, because these are the kind of people who will make you rich. You have to leverage and harness the intellectual strength and talent of these people. Intellectuals consist of professionals such as accountants, legal advisors, tax consultants, etc. They fill the gaps in your knowledge. Their intellectual strength helps you grow rich.

Microsoft Corporations grew mainly due to its ability to harness the intellectual strength of young computer whiz-kids on its pay roll. If Microsoft can do it, why can't you?

Leverage Other People's Time and Effort

All of us are born with different talents and proclivities. Some have a higher IQ, others are taller or better looking. But all of us have one thing which is universal, and that is time. All of us, without any exceptions, have only 24 hours in a day. It goes without saying that to be successful we have to leverage our time.

Most people look for job security rather than opportunity. They will sell their time, effort, resources and connections for a very low price. Wealth creators leverage the time and effort of others to generate wealth for themselves. This is the simplest form of leverage in labor intensive industries.

In fact, most businesses in today's world are founded on other people's time and effort.

"People without leverage work for those with leverage." – Robert Kiyosaki

If you are an employee, your company is leveraging your time and effort to increase their profits. It may sound cruel but it is the truth. This has been happening since the dawn of civilization. It is high time you started thinking of breaking out of this cycle and empowering yourself by using other people's time and effort to build your wealth.

You have to become a master at offloading routine jobs; to free up your time to concentrate on areas that are more creative and will help you create wealth faster. I am amused by people who are so self-efficient that they will not trust another human being even with the most mundane jobs, because they do not trust their competence. This is the sure route to stagnate.

To succeed and progress in life, you have to find people to replace your management and skillset in the shortest possible time frame.

How to Grow Rich with The Power of Leverage

You have to use the effort and energy of others to grow rich. This might be as simple as hiring someone to clean your house, mow your lawn, dry clean and press your shirt or hiring technical people to do your routine jobs at work. You should first write down and offload your bottom 10 routine activities (you don't enjoy doing,) that take up your time and energy from productive work, which in turn, can generate revenue for you.

You have only 24 hours in a day. No matter how talented or efficient you are, you can earn only a limited amount of money if you are paid by the hour. With a 40-hour work-week you can, at best, work for only 2000 hours in a year (assuming you take a 2-week vacation time and work 50 weeks).

If you employ, let us say, 100 people in your business, your work output will be 200,000 man-hours and your income that much higher

"I would rather earn 1% off 100 people's efforts than 100% of my own efforts." – John Paul Getty

You can also benefit from a percentage of other people's efforts and dramatically increase your income and freedom by learning to leverage your time.

"He who stands on the giants' shoulders; sees farther than the giant" - Puissant

To apply this technique, great human and management skills are needed. If you lack management skills; a more practical and pragmatic approach is to outsource jobs that need co-ordination of human skills. In this way, you avoid the hassle of managing people.

Leveraging Technology

Technology allows us to do things with greater precision, more efficiently and faster than ever before. Today, computers can process data and calculate results that needed hundred and thousands of man-hours. Similarly, the internet can provide access to information that would have taken hundreds of hours to research and collate.

Emails, modern telecommunications and internet have revolutionized communication. These technologies, when mastered, give leverage in terms of quality and speed of decision making—and they help save time and effort, thus resulting in huge cost savings. They are also impacting how we network, socially interact and conduct our businesses. To create wealth in today's world, one has to master leveraging these new technological advances.

To use this leverage, you have to be open to technology and buy the best of what your pocket allows.

I was privileged to be able to hear Bill Gates lecture at a conference in the early nineties. He emphasized on the importance of computers in our lives, especially that little extra technological edge that our children receive in this competitive world. At the time I had a computer at work, but not one at home. I was planning to buy one, but the high cost prohibited me from doing so back in those days. I was continuously delaying my decision to buy—the prices were regressing with every passing month and I was waiting for the appropriate moment to buy.

After attending that Bill Gates lecture, I went straight to a computer store and bought a PC for our home use—it was the best decision I ever made in my life! That PC not only helped me leverage my time and knowledge, but also gave my children an opportunity to grow up with the technological edge.

Since then, I have developed a habit of upgrading technology at home and at work: computers, mobile devices, communication systems, access to fast speed networks, etc. Access to information and sharing it with your customers provides the best possible leverage, in terms of customer relationship, sales and profits.

I have given an example of information technology for the ease of understanding, as it affects our day to day life; there are many other machines that replace human functions more efficiently and at a much cheaper cost. For instance, robots are able to assemble cars with more precision and in much lesser time than human beings. The fastest growing companies on our planet are those that are making technological breakthroughs on a regular basis in their respective fields. *Apple* is one such company.

Technology leverages work only when applied productively. There are people who waste time surfing the net endlessly, playing video games, socializing or using it only as source of entertainment. Nothing wrong indulging in such activities because we all need to keep informed and entertained – the problem is when lose we lose focus and become obsessed with it and spend endless hours socializing.

How to Grow Rich with The Power of Leverage

To create wealth you have to apply leverage of technology to your advantage rather than get lost in technology indulgence.

Social Media Leveraging

Social media platforms like Facebook, Twitter, YouTube and LinkedIn are the latest technological breakthroughs that are changing the way we do businesses and leverage ourselves. Viral marketing has taken up a new connotation due to the leverage provided by social media.

Unknown talents are discovered each day and made famous by the power of these viral information sharing platforms. These platforms are creating instant millionaires of those who know how to harness this new technological wave.

To apply maximum leverage, you have to use and market technologies that are most efficient and cutting edge.

Leveraging of Networks

"It's not what you know but who you know that makes the difference" Anonymous

A key contact can 'make it happen'. If you know the right person, things happen. The key contact is crucial to your success. He is the leverage that will work wonders for you. The value of a large network is that the chances of finding the right contact increase exponentially.

To succeed, you need the power of a large network. There are people who control large networks. You have to know who these people are in order to gain access to their networks. For example, if you are marketing a product, it is far easier to find one contact who controls a large network and market your product through him rather than selling your product independently to thousands of unconnected buyers.

The trick is to know either how to build a network or have some access to people who control networks. Understanding the power of networking is a very important leveraging tool.

If you wish to create wealth fast, then you have to master the art of networking. By forming a network of nurtured relationships, you get support, information, referrals, advice and access to resources.

It is your contacts who make you rich. If you know the industry leaders, you receive important information before anyone else—if you know the bankers, you get access to finance...if you are friends with your boss, you get promoted. The list is endless.

Cavett Robert, the dean of American speakers, rightly put it: *"you have to make contacts to get contracts"*. Your net worth will be equal to the size of your network.

You don't create a network by simply capturing names, telephone numbers and email addresses into your address book or database; you create a network by building a meaningful relationship over a period of time with the people who can trust you. The way to do this is to help everyone within your sphere of influence to the best of your ability. If you go an extra mile, you will put the Universe in your debt that will be repaid to you a hundred times over.

The best relationships are formed when you participate in someone's growth with the attitude of making them strong and independent. If you help people with the aim of getting something in return, to make them dependent on you financially or emotionally, then that relationship will not last for long. A plant can never grow under the shadow of a big tree.

You have to give something away for free that is of value to your network, to build relationships. This act of giving will foster trust and bring attention to you. Do not expect reciprocity in return or the value of your gift is lost.

The return you get for your free gift is trust and recognition. This will result in strengthening the foundation of your network and give it the longevity it needs.

The golden rule of networking is:

"Be very quick to build connections and extremely slow to break them" Robert G Allen

Your network will collapse if more people are leaving it as compared to those who are joining. To sustain your network, you have to keep adding value.

How to build a large Network quickly

To build a huge network, it is not a necessary condition for you to know thousands of people, to begin with. You initially have to start building a network by adding one person at a time. This is a very slow process at the beginning, but as you add value to your network, more people will gravitate towards it through word-of-mouth advertising or referrals. Sooner than later, key contacts who have large networks of their own will start taking note of your network.

And before you know it, you will find a key contact that controls a large network of people. To build a large network, you don't have to find just one key contact but several key contacts. The value of your network is the square of the number of people in it.

To find your key contact you will need to network with a large number of people; this will increase the possibility of finding the one key contact that will not only increase the size, but also the value of your network hundred-fold. The only way to build a large network is through consistency.

Examine your list of contacts critically and focus on those who have large networks and yield the maximum influence—make a special effort to build relationships with them and spend your time maintaining them. If they endorse your product or service to their database, your profits will multiply.

"Position yourself as the center of influence - the one who knows the movers and shakers. People will respond to that, and you'll soon become what you project."

The two aspects that increase the size of your network quickly are: what value you provide to your network and how many key contacts you can bring to your network.

You don't have to look too far; just look at the phenomenal growth of Google and Facebook! They provide invaluable services to their clients for free and as a result, have millions of subscribers joining them every month. This results in billions of dollars in revenue to these companies. If we can replicate even a little bit of their strategy in building our networks, we can become rich very quickly.

Weak Ties Network

Most people believe that it is important to have people whom they already know and have strong ties with, which will make their network stable and help it grow but nothing can be further from truth. It is your weak ties, or the people whom you don't know so well, that bring growth and new impetus to your network.

The reason for this is simple—the people who are close to you have much in common with you. They share the same value system, experiences and similar view points. The information they possess is already known to you and is of very little value to you. Your weak ties, on the other hand, bring fresh perspective and new ideas. It is imperative to keep in mind that it is your weak ties that add value to your network.

In addition to that, your weak ties will bring in a new circle of influence with their own set of friends and relatives to your network. In all likelihood, your inner circle of friends will not contribute towards the growth of your network to the same extent due to the limited number of new members they can add to your network.

The most influential people who will increase the size of your network are the 'connectors,' who are masters of those weak ties. These connectors have the energy, the self-confidence and the social attributes to connect with a large number of people—their special gifts create large networks of weak ties.

Either you must master connecting with the weak ties or with the connectors, who will bring weak ties to your network.

Networking the Networks

Another way of growing your network fast is by 'Networking the Networks.' There is a high number of existing networks in related fields that you can interact with to work towards a mutual advantage. Once you have built a network of considerable size, you can collaborate with other networks. This works in a similar way as the 'weak ties network.'

To give an example, if you have a network of real estate investor clients, it may be worth your while to collaborate with a mortgage broker who has a network of clients who borrow money to fund their real estate. You can also collaborate with accountants and attorneys who have a database of real estate investor clients—by giving cross referrals, all the key players can increase the size of their networks.

These days, it is relatively easy to find related networks by doing a search on the internet and building a relationship with the key players in those networks. The people who operate large networks understand the importance of increasing the size of their network by collaborating with other networks. So, don't be shy in approaching these people.

Metcalf's Law

"The value of a network grows in proportion to the square of the number of users"

An average person will know around, at least, 200 people. Each of those 200 people will have their own sphere of influence and will also know 200 people. So, if you build a network of 200 people, you will have access to over 200x200 (40,000 people.)

If you take this one step further, those 40,000 people will have their own spheres of influence of 200 people each—the possibilities are endless!

It is therefore critical that you start building your network with integrity as you sit at the center of your sphere of influence. If you try and fake your network, you will not succeed. Keep adding value to your network without any expectations of return, and watch your network grow.

Centre of Influence

Always remember that you are the center of influence in your network. Even if you have a great dream-team, you remain the leader of your team that will exert the key influence in creating your network.

You have to develop the traits that help influence your network: you have to make yourself immensely likable and radiate positive energy, and your personality and eye contact should radiate warmth and friendliness. Develop a personality that is always looking to help others grow in whatever their endeavor or goal may be in life, and always be willing to give and add value without any hope of reciprocity—that will make your influence grow.

Integrity, integrity, integrity. There is no substitute for integrity. Never promote an idea, service or goods to your network that you are not using or have doubts about. You cannot fake and build a network. Be yourself and act honestly. You will attract the right kind of people into your network, which will help you grow in leaps and bounds with their support.

Ethical leverage is essential in networking. You have to use your contacts wisely. If you try and use your contacts without thought of return on everyone's time and effort, then you may succeed in lifting your load, but your strategy, in the long run, will fail. Your network will collapse.

I get hundreds of emails every month from internet marketers trying to promote affiliate products. It is very easy to find out a fake promotion coming from a person who has never used a product or has very little knowledge about it. I immediately unsubscribe from the list of those who try and promote such products. On the other hand, I continue to be on the list of those who email me information that is of value to me and, at times, buy products on their recommendation.

How to Grow Rich with The Power of Leverage

The power of leverage comes from using your networking skills wisely. There are two fundamental rules to networking:

• **Pay It Forward-** Assist 3 people to succeed and in return of what you do for them, request them to help 3 others. This is leverage.

• **Share the Rewards** – Share the rewards of your success and prosperity with all those who are involved in your network.

If you are honest, genuine and helpful your sphere of influence and network will grow. Your network, if built correctly, will, without a doubt, make you rich.

Leveraging Systems

The ultimate aim of any income stream is to make it work on autopilot or with minimal supervision from you. This can only be achieved by putting proper systems in place so that it can function without your intervention. This is the ultimate leverage that will free up your time and effort to devote to other important things in life such as family, travel, leisure, creativity or other ventures that will create new sources of wealth for you.

When I was in the Navy, we had a saying that it was a system designed by a genius to be run by fools. All the procedures were laid out for us to the last detail. We knew what action to take in an emergency, what logs and forms to fill up, how to demand stores, etc. When an order was given to 'dive' or 'surface,' every crew member who was on-board the submarine knew exactly what action to take. Nothing was left to chance.

A well-run income stream or business should be run in a similar manner. The problem is that most of us know how to work within a system designed by others but are clueless when it comes to designing a system for our own work or business.

The answer to this problem is to buy into a system that is very closely related to your work and adapt them to your requirement. An alternate solution is to work with an expert who has the skills to design and set up systems.

To leverage our time and effort, we have to be on a constant lookout for setting up systems to free our effort and time. These can be very straightforward things like: setting up automatic online payments for our bills or more sophisticated automated systems to put our business in auto pilot. There may be some cost and effort involved to initially set up the systems, but once they are in place, they free up your energy to do more creative work. The aim of any good system is to take care of the routine work thereby leveraging time and effort for creative work.

To become rich, you need to have proper systems in place–QED. Without SYTEMS, you are doomed to failure. Research has shown that 94% of the failures are not due to the assumption that people don't do a good job, but because either they are using the wrong business systems or have no systems in place to start with.

For the ease of understanding, the right acronym for systems is:

Save **Y**our **S**elf **T**ime **E**nergy **M**oney

If you want to make money, then search and find a money-making vehicle that has successful systems. You will save time, energy and money if you have systems in place before you embark on money-making ventures. If you don't have the skills to set up systems, then buy into business/ investment ventures that have systems in place. Every enlightened wealth creator knows this simple truth. They buy into time-tested predictable systems that will do the job for them. That is why when initially starting your own business; it may be wiser to buy into a franchisee that has strong systems rather than building your own from scratch. Chances of failure will thus be reduced. As you gain experience, you can develop your own system.

Once you have systems in place, the system will churn out money for you. All the work is done upfront to set up the system. You will only need to fine-tune it, once in operation, to make it work optimally.

Characteristics of an Ideal Money-Making System

Zero Time

This means that once you have a project up and running, it should run more or less on autopilot and require minimum time intervention from you.

I am a property investor and I treat each property as a separate money-making stream of income. My process is very simple; I buy family homes with surplus land to build a second house on it. I focus on properties that are being sold at a price that is, at least, 15-20% below market value and aim towards a long-term settlement.

Delayed settlement gives me time to get all the clearances from the City Council for building plans and renovations. At times, I also get capital appreciation even before I have settled.

I then try and make renovations to the older house so as to increase its rent. I also contract reputed builders to build a second house on the additional land—thereby increasing the cash flow further. These two actions along-with delayed settlement increase the value of the property by 20-30% and give me cash flow in excess of 10%.

Once the project is completed, I hand over the property to a competent property manager. I never manage a property myself. I make sure that my investment-properties have adequate cash flow to pay the mortgage, expenses and the property management costs. This frees up my time to do the next project.

There have been times when I do not exchange a single phone-call with my property manager for a whole year. Once a project is completed, properties bring in money on autopilot without my interventions. I then move on to my next project and repeat the whole process. The increase in equity from buying low and adding value gives me money to use as down payment for the next property.

This method of investing in property is only an example. You can buy into proven franchises or self-perpetuating viral programs on the internet that take very little of your time, once they are set up correctly. The goal is to build a massive amount of passive income with little or no investment of your time.

Zero Out Of Pocket Money

Columbus borrowed money for his expedition from the royal family of Spain. Discovery of Americas brought huge returns for Columbus regarding recognition and finances.

You will need money to fund your investment or business. You have to find systems to get the funding from outside and use little or no money of your own.

In real estate, you must have heard of 'Nothing Down' deals. It is fairly common for sophisticated investors to buy properties with no money of their own. Even if they have to put money into a deal, they try and take out their investment at the first opportunity available.

Zero Risk

Once you learn to do investments and business without putting your personal money into a deal, then your risk is virtually zero.

Many will argue that 'No Money Deals' increase the amount of leverage and the risk of bankruptcy. Sophisticated investors set up corporations and other legal entities to protect themselves from any adverse fallout and limit their liability if something untoward happens.

The more sophisticated you become as an investor your risk management skills to put right systems in place to avoid/ minimize risks will improve.

Zero Management

You have to be constantly on the lookout to find systems and technology to replace yourself. To go to the next, higher level of income, you have to keep finding competent people and systems to replace you.

You have to master the art of outsourcing and delegation. You have to find businesses and investments with systems in place that take up the least of your time and effort. Most people forget to take into account the cost of management time and base their business and investment decisions purely on ROI (rate of return). This can have disastrous results in the long run as it will not only impede your financial growth, but also have adverse effects on your health, family time and relationships.

Robert Allen, in his book One Minute Millionaire, justly states, "*You have to learn to ZERO OUT your life*" in order to succeed.

Caution about Leveraging

Leveraging is a great way of creating accelerated wealth but it comes with a warning: if leveraging is applied incorrectly it can destroy your wealth equally fast.

The higher the leverage, the greater is the risk to your investment and business. At the same time, there is greater potential for profits. Leverage works both ways; it is a double-edged sword.

Before applying leverage, you have to understand some basic truths about leveraging or things could go dramatically wrong and you can get yourself hurt and go bankrupt.

State of Knowledge

The financial crisis of 2008 was caused when excessive greed led people to use leverage without proper understanding of risks involved. The most important factor for using leverage correctly is your state of knowledge.

For instance, if you lack knowledge about finances or the business/investment you wish to start, there is no point in rushing to get 100% finance in order to try making a no-money-down deal.

Similarly, if you lack the knowledge of systems and how to set them up, there is no point in rushing to fully automate your operations. Same is true for any form of leveraging.

You should make a correct assessment of your financial, emotional and spiritual knowledge in any given situation before applying leverage as an instrument for accelerated wealth creation. Greed is the product of a lacking emotional and spiritual intelligence. Leverage driven by greed is the worst enemy of wealth creation.

Leverage is like a power tool that can make your job of wealth creation very easy but its improper use, without adequate knowledge or precautions, can cause you tremendous hurt.

There is a saying that, '***It is never the investment that is wrong. It is always the investor who is wrong***'. So, take the time and trouble to learn about the business or investment before jumping onto the bandwagon of leveraging for quick gains.

Market Conditions

In uncertain market conditions, when the outcome is not known or when the market is moving downwards, the amount of leverage should be reduced.

How to Grow Rich with The Power of Leverage

You could increase the leverage as you gain confidence, and when the market forces are moving in a positive direction.

For example, in property investment, it is extremely easy to do 'no money down deals' if you have the right knowledge and the market is moving up. This is because even if you make a mistake, the rise in price of the property will cover your error. On the other hand, doing a low equity deal when the property cycle is moving southward then even a small error in your judgment will wipe out your equity.

If you are using leverage for accelerated financial returns, then you have to be very alert towards changing market conditions. If the market conditions deteriorate, then you have to take measures to reduce your leverage in time. People go bankrupt when they hesitate to act or foresee a developing situation. Reducing your leverage by selling some of your assets is no shame. You can always buy assets and increase your leverage when favorable market conditions return.

Age Factor

The amount of leverage to apply is also dependent your age. When you are young, you can risk applying high levels of leverage. This is because even if things go wrong, you have the time to recover and start all over again. Once you age time is not on your side and if things go wrong there is no time to recover and restart.

As you grow older, it is wise to reduce leverage even if you have become more proficient at applying leverage with experience. The last remark will, no doubt, be debated because there are many elderly people who are still young at heart and ready to take all kinds of risks in life. I, unfortunately, speak for the majority.

Risk Appetite

Before applying leverage, you have to access your risk appetite. This is because if things go wrong, then people with less risk appetite will start to panic and make incorrect decisions that can set them back by years in their financial growth and planning.

Greed

Greed is the biggest enemy of leverage. It is greed which makes us blind to applying leverage without appropriate knowledge, skills and timing. Before applying leverage, one has to develop checks and balances provided by spiritual, financial and emotional intelligence.

How to Maximize Leverage

Acquire a Mentor

You can avoid making mistakes on the learning curve by finding a mentor who can guide you through the whole process. Your mentor has climbed the mountain—he knows the terrain and knows what works and what does not work. You can learn from the process and avoid making mistakes.

In addition, your mentor has systems. The most efficient facet of leverage is to transfer your mentor's systems to your use. Learn from those systems and apply those systems to your business, real estate, stock market and internet.

Acquire a Team

Nature made us incomplete—we have incomplete knowledge and experience; we have to collaborate and build dream-teams to fill gaps in our knowledge and competence to succeed. Our teams can fill up our blind spots.

If you want accelerated leverage then find a competent team to help you. Your team will help you go faster. A 4X100 meter relay team runs much faster than an individual runner.

Your team can consist of people with expert knowledge in their respective fields. They don't have to be your employees but should be available for advice. For instance, if you are a real estate investor your team will consist of your accountant, solicitor, and real estate agents who bring you deals, mortgage broker and your builder/ handyman. If these people are property investors, they will be able to give you better quality advice.

Before you start building your network, find your core groups that will help you build your network. When likeminded, joyful and success-oriented people work together, enormous energy is released. Try and avoid people with negative energy around them—they will drag you down.

Your core group or dream-team will provide the synergy to create an invisible force that will attract people to your network. 1 + 1 is, not 2, but 11. The sum of the parts is far greater than the whole. This is what your core group can help you achieve.

Jesus selected a core group of 12 men, and the world was never the same again. Their network and influence has lasted over centuries and continues to expand even today.

Bill Gates and Paul Allen collaborated to found Microsoft and became the richest men of all times. Larry Page and Sergey Brin founded Google that is used by millions of users and is presently expanding incessantly.

Facebook, which is the biggest networking platform of all times, was created by a team of four Harvard University students: Mark Zuckerberg, Dustin Moskovitz, Eduardo Saverin and Chris Huges. The examples that history provide are endless.

A core group constituted of an aligning team (that is not pulling in different directions) will always out-perform an individual. So, don't try to do it alone. Build a core group first and then your network.

Loverage

Mike Littman coined the term 'Loverage'. If you love what you are doing and are spiritually and emotionally connected with it, then success will come much easily. When your thoughts, mind, body, emotions and spiritual self are congruent you achieve unassailable heights.

Ask any sportsperson about their greatest sporting moments, and you'll find them acknowledge that at the height of their achievement, their mind, body and spirit dissolve into a singular force. Do what you love doing and you will apply the 'Loverage' even without knowing.

Final Thoughts on Leverage

There is no such thing as a hundred percent leverage. It is a myth perpetuated by certain vested individuals who want to market their books and products. There will always be some financial, time, and effort commitment in the beginning. In due course, as the business or investment progresses, finance and time involvement can be reduced, and leverage increased.

The above arguments should not dissuade you from using leverage with prudence and intelligence. Leverage, without doubt, is the most important and powerful tool in the armory of wealth creators. However, it is of paramount importance to understand its correct usage before applying it in a fit of excitement. Initially, start applying small forms of leverage and as your confidence grows, you can increase the amount of leverage to one that you are comfortable with.

Even if you start applying a little bit of leverage in your life, you will be amazed at the results. Leverage is power, strength and intelligence.

Mark Victor Hansen and Robert Allen, in their book 'One Minute Millionaire,' provided a formula:

Leverage = Speed = Goals

This, in my view, sums up how you can use leverage to reach your financial goals within the shortest period of time. You can increase your returns from 5-10% offered by banks and financial institutions to over 60-70%, or even higher through leveraging.

Remember, without applying some kind of leverage, there is no possibility of creating accelerated wealth.

Multiple Streams of Income

Once you learn the use of leverage to run your businesses/ investments you will be able to create multiple streams of income with ease. This is because none of businesses require your time or physical intervention.

You develop one income stream, put it on auto, free up your time and look for another opportunity to build another source of passive income.

Keep repeating the process—this will provide you with financial safety and stability. It will also reduce your risk. In case, one income source dries up, you have several others working for you. Never become content nor rely on one source of income.

The purpose of this book will be served if it helps in educating and help morph enlightened people who create wealth the right way, preserve wealth the right way and ultimately, use their wealth for the greater good of humanity. This process leads to seeking a higher purpose in life and its fulfillment. I hope and pray that to some extent, that purpose is served. If you have read to this point, I thank you with gratitude in my heart and hope you succeed in creating true wealth that helps not only you and your family but entire humanity.

If you liked the book and gained some knowledge that will be useful to you in life, then please leave an honest review to help others find this book. It will be a small effort on your part, but an act of charity that may help in changing few lives for the better. I thank you in advance for your help.

This book is about fundamental principles of wealth creation that can be applied to any business or investing strategy. At <u>Wealth Creation Academy</u>, we teach multitude ways to generate passive income, which includes: real estate investing, digital publishing, affiliate marketing, multi-level marketing and investing in forex, commodities, and shares by copying experienced traders that need very little of time. You may like to get started with some of the strategies depending on your budget and time.

Other Books by the Author

Praveen Kumar has authored several bestselling books. Please visit his website http://praveenkumarauthor.com/ for more information

About the Authors

Praveen Kumar was abandoned by his father at the age of fourteen and joined the Navy at tender age of fifteen where education, roof and free food were guaranteed.

In order to understand the root cause of suffering he turned towards philosophy and religion. After 10 years of soul searching and meditation he understood that 'life is 'and material and spiritual world are closely interwoven. You cannot live in one without the other.

Praveen was highly successful in the Navy, where he successfully commanded submarines, sailed around the world in a yacht and received gallantry award for his contribution to the Navy.

Despite his success in the Navy, Praveen realized that lack of financial security for his family was one of key root causes of his suffering, resulting from his childhood deprivation. To improve his financial standing, Praveen took pre-mature retirement from the Navy to build his financial future through investing in Real Estate. The decision to educate on financial matters paid off, and today he and his wife are comfortably retired on six-figure passive income.

His aim is to help others create wealth in an enlightened way and empower them to live a healthy and happy life. He dedicates his time to write books and articles on financial and spiritual matters.

Prashant graduated with distinction from Auckland University as a computer engineer and later completed his MBA from the world's leading institution - INSEAD. During his successful corporate career, he worked for the most reputable consulting firms in the world - BCG & Deloitte - and represented New Zealand on Prime

Minister-led trade missions to South East Asian countries.

After successfully generating income through his passive investments in property and stocks, Prashant decided to team up with his father to help people transform their lives through the leverage of financial education.

Their website http://wealth-creation-academy.com/ is devoted to teaching people how to create Multiple Streams of Passive Income through investing in real estate, online marketing and creating digital products